# A selected antholog

## by


# Cornelius O'Hamster-McFishpants

# Contents

## Preamble

This book represents some of the poems I am most proud of, from the 9,364 I have written over my 64¾ years on this planet. My poems are observational, based on things I see in my everyday life, dreams I have had, or fantasies I have entertained. I hope you enjoy them!

COM, Basildon, January 2024

## A dream

I had a dream the other day

There was a whale in it

The whale was quite sexy

And tumescent

I awoke and the sheets were damp

Which was curious, as I had not shit myself.

## On the jilter of an unnamed member of the royal family

I was in a Pizza Express

Sweating

When to my surprise

Some jilter appeared on my elbow

Salty, yet sweet

Fragrant with vanilla and lemon.

# My thoughts on dogshit

Is it wrong

That I often think of dogshit?

The old white ones were the best

But the brown ones are also nice

I find it hard to resist

Dipping a finger in, and having a taste.

## A poem about horses

I find horses very sexually attractive

I do not know if it is the proudness of their bearing or the size of their tumescence.

## What about jacksies?

Asked the bishop to the actress

As they drunkenly

Fondled behind the bins at the Basildon branch of a discount supermarket.

# Colonoscopies

I have never had a colonoscopy

I have often thought I would like to

To see what I look like on the inside

I imagine proud, defiant and primed for action

But my GP tells me I am wasting his time and to fuck off.

# Is it OK to be naked when taking the bins out?

My local policeman said not, but I think a debate can be had here

I just greatly enjoy the jiggling of my member when pushing the wheelie

over the gravelstones of my driveway

And cheekily mooning by neighbour Bradley

While he is enjoying his morning coffee.

## On the jilter of a major, now shamed, TV celebrity

I expect that it tastes golden

Like rainbows and unicorns

Thick, gelatinous and gloopy

Running from the table to the floor.

# What is ham?

Delicious meat

Lovesock

Carpet

Lubricant

Sandwich filler

Husband?

## My favourite song

Is hard to choose

I love all the works of Michael Bubbly

But also Craig David

And Cliff Richard

If only they all formed a supergroup and recorded a song about koalas.

# What should I do with my old sex toys?

I was thinking of putting them in the bin

But to be honest they are a bit shitted up

From having been up my bottom

And the bottom of my friends

So maybe I should wash them first?

I tried to get the dog to lick them clean, but that did not work.

## Should I cuddle him?

The man in the pub next to me

Reading the Sunday Sport and drinking tequila?

I would like to

Though he smells of wee.

# A friend in the north

Sexy

Tall

Monksexy

I have often wondered if he works as a stripper at the weekends.

## Cats

Brown

Black

Orange

Occasionally left unattended.

# A poem Bard wrote about fishmongers and camels

In briny air where scales still gleam,

The fishmonger holds his watery realm.

Cod stacked like coins, eyes wide and glassy,

Salmon slices, coral pink and classy.


A cry rings out, "Oysters fresh today!"

Shucked pearls beneath the sea-salt spray.

Lobsters claw the icy air,

While crabs scuttle, caught unawares.


But in the desert's golden hush,

Where sand dunes dance and mirages brush,

A different merchant plies his trade,

His wares not caught, but gently led.


Camels kneel, burdened with spice,

Silk threads that shimmer, ivory dice.

Their humps, like ships, bear treasures untold,

Frankincense, myrrh, and stories bold.


From ocean's depths to scorching sand,

These merchants bind two distant lands.

One with ocean's salty song,

The other where wind whispers all night long.

But both with calloused hands they meet,

Trading whispers, bitter and sweet.

Of sun-baked sands and waves that crash,

Of life's bounty, borne on land and splash.


So let us raise a toast, a briny sip,

To fishmongers, camels, and the trade they clip.

For in their journey, vast and wide, they weave a world where waters

divide.

## A poem Bard wrote about slamdunks, haddock, and crochet

With sneakers squeaking, a symphony's beat,

He flies through the air, defying gravity's feat.

A leather orb soars, a fiery arc it traces,

Then slams in the hoop, a net-rippling embrace.


But when hardwood sleeps, and adrenaline wanes,

He turns to softer crafts, where patience reigns.

Haddock, flaky white, lays chilled on the board,

As nimble fingers weave a fishy accord.


Each stitch a loop, a yarn-spun scale it paints,

Transforming scales to finery, saints.

A haddock mandala, swimming in white,

A fishy halo, shimmering day and night.

Then yarn of teal, and emerald green ignite,

A Granny square blooms, a sea-foam delight.

Coral bubbles pop, anemones unfurl,

A crocheted reef, unfurling from the world.

Slamdunks to stitches, a rhythm untold,

Two passions dance, both fierce and bold.

For creativity's flame burns in many a guise,

In leaps and loops, where heart and hand conspire.

So raise a yarn ball, a haddock fin on high,

To the artist's spirit, soaring to the sky.

In dunks and stitches, a soul takes flight,

A tapestry woven, day and starry night.

## A poem Bard wrote about supplication and the art of ironmongery

In shadowed naves, where tapers sigh,

And prayers like smoke ascend the sky,

I kneel, a supplicant in chains,

To gods of gears and tempered reins.


No incense burns, no hymns resound,

But clanging hammer, anvil bound,

These forge-born hymns my spirit raise,

A symphony of molten praise.


The blacksmith's hand, a holy rite,

Transforms raw ore to tempered light,

In tongs He grasps, in fire He dips,

And form from chaos gently lips.


The bellows wheeze, a whispered plea,

The molten heart bleeds molten sea,

Each spark a prayer, each clang a vow,

To mend the broken, build anew.


From nails that bind, to gates that swing,

His ironed grace makes offerings,

Chains unfurled, to plowshares wrought,

Redemption forged, from battles fought.

And in the hush, when hammer sleeps,

The ironmonger's wisdom keeps,

In tempered blade and weathered key,

The whispered secrets set men free.


So let me kneel, in workshop dim,

Where supplication's smoky hymn

Ascends on sparks, in clang and sigh,

To gods of iron, 'neath the sky.

## A poem Bard wrote about accidentally spilling marmite on one's lover

In love's embrace, on sourdough toast,
A midnight snack, a lover's ghost,
We slathered spread, a dark delight,
Marmite's magic, setting things alight.

But oh, the crumbs, a treacherous dance,
A rogue yeast flake, took sudden chance,
And like a rogue yeast comet's trail,
Marmite splattered, love did wail.

Her chin, a canvas, stained and bold,
A sticky map, a story told,
Of midnight feasts and laughter's spray,
And marmite mishaps, come what may.

His grin, a sheepish, yeasty charm,
Disarmed the sting, dispelled the alarm,
"My love," he chuckled, "war paint bold,
A warrior queen, in marmite gold."

With fingers warm, and laughter's brush,
He traced the map, a gentle hush,
And on her cheek, a smudged reply,
A mirrored stain, beneath the sky.

So clink the mugs, let marmite flow,

Though love gets sticky, hearts still glow,

For in the mess, the mishaps made,

Love's truest test, is marmalade.

# A poem Bard wrote about wrestling

In kitchen bright, where sunlight streamed,
A battle brewed, no swords were dreamed.
No clash of steel, no thundering might,
Just Jon and Timmy, locked in fight.

A vat of crimson, wobbling, sweet,
Strawberry jelly, ankle-deep.
Grinning wide, with cherry stains,
They plunged within, no fear, no gains.

Jon, a hulk of man, with doughy fists,
A playful glint in sun-kissed mists.
Timmy, nimble, quick as thought,
Through jiggly waves, his laughter caught.

They grappled, oozing, sticky forms,
Strawberry rivers, berry storms.
Elbows sunk, then popped with glee,
A squishy symphony, you see.

Jon, a barge, Timmy, darting eel,
A fruity dance, their senses reel.
Jelly plops, a chorus sung,
As laughter danced on every tongue.

Plunges deep, like berry dives,
Strawberry spray on giggling eyes.
No winner crowned, no loser there,
Just joyous mess, with sticky hair.

From kitchen floor to jelly tide,
They rolled and splashed, with open wide.
A fruity war, a sugary scene,
Jon and Timmy, jelly kings, serene.

So next time boredom clouds your day,
Don't fight with toys, don't run away.
Just grab some berries, red and sweet,
And dive in deep, with jelly feat.

For in the squish, the giggles rise,
A sticky friendship, sweet surprise.
For Jon and Timmy, hand in hand,
Found joy in jelly, wonderland.